AI Engineering for Beginners: A Practical Guide to Building Intelligent Systems from the Ground Up

James Douglas

Book Cover by James Douglas

1st edition 2025

Introduction

Welcome to the world of AI engineering—a world where machines don't just follow instructions, but learn, adapt, and help us solve problems in entirely new ways.

This book is designed for curious minds. You might be a beginner with no formal background in computer science. Maybe you've dabbled in Python, or maybe you've only heard the buzzwords—machine learning, neural networks, deep learning—and wondered what it all means. Wherever you're starting from, this book will guide you step by step through the landscape of modern AI engineering.

You'll learn how to build your first models, work with real data, understand essential tools, and, most importantly, think critically about the ethical and practical implications of deploying AI in the real world.

Let's begin.

Contents

1

What Is AI Engineering?

1. Understanding the Basics

Imagine you're building a robot that can play chess—not just any robot, but one that can improve its strategy over time. You could, in theory, write thousands of lines of code dictating every possible move and scenario. But eventually, you'd hit a wall. There are more possible chess games than atoms in the universe. You'd be programming forever. That's where **artificial intelligence** steps in—not as a set of rules written by humans, but as systems that learn from data and experience.

What is Artificial Intelligence?

Artificial Intelligence (AI) refers to the broad field of building systems that can perform tasks that would normally require human intelligence. These tasks include recognizing speech, making decisions, understanding natural language, spotting patterns in data, and even driving cars or composing music. AI doesn't mean creating human-like consciousness (though Hollywood might like us to think that). Most of what we call "AI" today is better understood as highly trained pattern recognition.

There are many flavors of AI—from rule-based systems that mimic decision trees to more sophisticated models like deep neural networks that learn from mountains of data. What ties them together is the goal: enabling machines to learn, reason, and adapt.

How AI Differs from Traditional Programming

Traditional programming is like writing a very detailed recipe. You tell the computer *exactly* what to do, step by step. For instance, if you were programming a thermostat, you might write: "If the temperature drops below 68°F, turn on the heat." Simple cause and effect.

AI flips this approach. Instead of writing the rules, you give the system *examples* and let it infer the rules. You show it hundreds of thousands of pictures of cats and dogs, label them, and the system learns what makes a cat a cat and a dog a dog. The result isn't a list of rules—it's a model that can generalize and make predictions on new data.

This shift—from explicit instructions to learned behavior—is what makes AI both powerful and unpredictable. It's why AI systems sometimes surprise us with cleverness... or fail in baffling ways.

AI Engineering vs. AI Research

So where does **AI engineering** fit in?

Think of AI research as the world of theory, experimentation, and innovation. Researchers are the ones inventing new algorithms, exploring the limits of what machines can learn, and publishing papers on cutting-edge breakthroughs.

AI engineering, by contrast, is about making AI work in the real world. It's practical, systems-focused, and product-driven. Engineers take those theoretical advances and translate them into robust, scalable applications—recommendation engines, fraud detectors, chatbots, medical diagnostics, and more.

In short: researchers *ask* if something is possible. Engineers *make* it possible.

2. The Role of an AI Engineer

You don't have to be a math prodigy or an algorithm wizard to become an AI engineer—but you do need to be curious, methodical, and comfortable with both software and data. AI engineering is a multidisciplinary role, combining elements of computer science, statistics, software engineering, and domain knowledge.

Key Responsibilities and Skill Sets

At its core, an AI engineer is responsible for designing, building, testing, and deploying AI models. This might include:

- Collecting and preparing data
- Training machine learning models
- Evaluating and tuning performance
- Integrating models into larger systems
- Monitoring models in production

The day-to-day can vary wildly depending on the project. One week you might be experimenting with a new deep learning architecture; the next, you're debugging a data pipeline or explaining model results to a stakeholder.

Key skills include:

- **Programming** (especially in Python)
- **Machine learning frameworks** (like TensorFlow or PyTorch)
- **Data wrangling** (using tools like Pandas, NumPy, SQL)
- **Model evaluation and validation**
- **Communication**, especially when translating technical concepts to non-technical teams

Common Tools and Technologies Used

AI engineers live in a vibrant ecosystem of tools. You'll likely encounter:

- **Jupyter Notebooks** for exploratory work
- **Scikit-learn** for traditional ML models
- **TensorFlow** and **PyTorch** for deep learning
- **Docker** and **Git** for deployment and version control
- **Cloud platforms** (AWS, Google Cloud, Azure) for scaling

The specific tools may evolve, but the underlying mindset—build, test, improve, repeat—remains constant.

Collaboration with Other Tech Roles

AI engineering isn't a solo endeavor. You'll collaborate with:

- **Data scientists**, who often lead the exploratory analysis and prototyping
- **Software engineers**, who help integrate AI into production systems
- **Product managers**, who define what needs to be built and why

- **UX designers**, who shape how users interact with AI-powered features

In many ways, AI engineers act as a bridge—translating raw data and abstract models into tangible, useful applications.

3. Why AI Engineering Matters

If you've ever had Netflix suggest a show you loved, or asked Siri for directions, or unlocked your phone with your face—you've already benefited from AI engineering. But beyond convenience, AI is increasingly woven into the fabric of critical systems around the world.

Real-World Applications

AI engineering is already making a profound impact across industries:

- **Healthcare**: AI helps detect diseases in X-rays, optimize treatment plans, and even predict patient deterioration.

- **Finance**: Banks use AI to flag fraudulent transactions and personalize financial recommendations.

- **Transportation**: From route optimization to autonomous vehicles, AI is transforming how we move.

- **Retail**: Inventory prediction, customer service chatbots, and dynamic pricing all rely on AI.

- **Climate science**: AI helps analyze satellite data, model weather patterns, and predict environmental changes.

These applications are only the tip of the iceberg. As models grow more capable and data becomes more abundant, the possibilities multiply.

Economic and Societal Impact

AI is already reshaping the job market—automating some roles, augmenting others, and creating entirely new career paths. Businesses that successfully harness AI see increased efficiency, better decision-making, and a competitive edge.

But the societal impact goes beyond business. AI systems influence decisions about loans, bail, hiring, and education. When designed well, they can promote fairness and accessibility. When designed poorly—or carelessly—they can reinforce bias and injustice.

That's why **AI engineering isn't just technical—it's ethical.**

The Need for Ethical and Responsible AI

Every AI engineer plays a role in shaping the behavior and impact of the systems they build. That means asking hard questions:

- Where is the data coming from?
- Who might be harmed by incorrect predictions?
- Is the model explainable, or a black box?

- What safeguards are in place to monitor its behavior?

Responsible AI isn't just a buzzword—it's a requirement. The best engineers don't just build models that *work*. They build models that *should* work.

In the next chapter, we'll break down the foundations of artificial intelligence and machine learning—covering key concepts, essential math and programming, and the role data plays in training intelligent systems.

Let's keep building.

2

Foundations of AI and Machine Learning

Before you can build intelligent systems, you need to understand what intelligence looks like when it's coded in lines of Python, trained on messy data, and evaluated by cold, hard metrics. This chapter lays the groundwork—not just for building models, but for *thinking* like an AI engineer.

We'll explore the major types of learning, peek under the hood of neural networks, and break down the essential math and programming concepts that power it all. And we'll talk about data—because data isn't just important in AI. It *is* AI.

1. Core Concepts of AI

Supervised, Unsupervised, and Reinforcement Learning

Machine learning isn't a single method—it's a toolbox. And inside that toolbox are three main drawers: **supervised**, **unsupervised**, and **reinforcement learning**. Each one teaches a machine in a slightly different way.

- **Supervised Learning** is like studying with an answer key. You give the algorithm labeled examples—say, images tagged "cat" or "dog"—and it learns to map inputs to correct outputs. This powers things like email spam filters, credit risk scoring, and voice recognition.

- **Unsupervised Learning** is more like giving a student a stack of books and asking them to group similar ones together without any labels. The algorithm finds patterns, clusters, or structures in the data. Use cases include customer segmentation, anomaly detection, and topic modeling.

- **Reinforcement Learning** is trial-and-error learning. The model interacts with an environment, receives feedback in the form of rewards or penalties, and learns to optimize its actions. Think of training a dog with treats—or teaching an AI to play chess or operate a robot arm.

Each learning type has its sweet spot. Supervised learning dominates most commercial applications, but reinforcement and unsupervised learning are gaining traction fast—especially in robotics, gaming, and recommendation systems.

Neural Networks and Deep Learning

A **neural network** is the backbone of most modern AI. Inspired (very loosely) by the brain, it consists of interconnected layers of nodes—called neurons—that transform input data into predictions.

Imagine trying to classify images as "cat" or "not cat." The input layer might receive raw pixel data. Hidden layers gradually detect patterns—edges, shapes, fur textures. The output layer finally says, "Yep, this looks like a cat."

Deep learning refers to networks with many hidden layers. These can model highly complex patterns and relationships, which is why deep learning powers image recognition, speech synthesis, and language translation.

Training a neural network involves:

- Feeding in data
- Making predictions
- Measuring how wrong it is (using a **loss function**)
- Adjusting the weights using **backpropagation** and **gradient descent**

It's a cycle of guess, measure, and improve—over thousands or millions of examples.

Natural Language Processing and Computer Vision

AI isn't just about numbers. It's about helping machines understand the world the way we do—through language and sight.

- **Natural Language Processing (NLP)** enables machines to understand, generate, and work with human language. Applications include chatbots, translation tools, sentiment analysis, and search engines.

- **Computer Vision** allows machines to interpret visual input—identifying objects, detecting movement, analyzing faces, and reading handwriting.

These subfields of AI often use deep learning models specialized for sequences (like **transformers** in NLP) or images (like **convolutional neural networks**, or CNNs).

The big idea? AI systems can now "see" and "read" in ways that mimic, and sometimes surpass, human abilities.

2. Essential Math and Programming

Let's get one thing out of the way: you don't need to be a math genius to succeed in AI. But understanding *how* and *why* things work will make you a better, more confident engineer.

Linear Algebra and Calculus Basics

At the heart of most machine learning is **linear algebra**—the study of vectors, matrices, and the operations you can perform on them. You'll use it to:

- Represent data as vectors or matrices

- Apply transformations (like rotations, scaling, or

projections)

- Compute dot products and matrix multiplications, which underpin model calculations

Calculus (mostly derivatives and gradients) helps you understand how models learn. **Gradient descent** uses calculus to figure out the direction to adjust model parameters so that prediction errors decrease.

You don't have to do these calculations by hand. Libraries like NumPy and PyTorch handle that. But knowing *why* they work will make debugging and model tuning far easier.

Probability and Statistics for ML

AI is about making predictions under uncertainty. That means probability and statistics are must-know topics.

Important concepts include:

- **Distributions** (normal, binomial, etc.)
- **Mean, variance, standard deviation**
- **Conditional probability and Bayes' theorem**
- **Confidence intervals and p-values**
- **Overfitting vs. generalization**

Statistics helps you evaluate model performance, avoid false conclusions, and build models that generalize well to new data.

Python and AI Libraries (NumPy, Pandas, Scikit-learn)

Python is the dominant language for AI engineering—thanks to its simplicity, readability, and the sheer number of high-quality libraries.

Key libraries to know:

- **NumPy**: For numerical computing with arrays and matrices
- **Pandas**: For working with structured data (like CSV files or tables)
- **Matplotlib / Seaborn**: For data visualization
- **Scikit-learn**: For training, testing, and evaluating traditional machine learning models

These libraries let you explore, clean, and model data without reinventing the wheel—and they're great for beginners and pros alike.

3. Introduction to Data

Data is the fuel of AI. It's how models learn patterns, make predictions, and improve over time. But not all data is created equal.

What Makes Data "AI-Ready"?

For data to be useful to an AI model, it should be:

- **Structured**: Clean rows and columns, consistent formats
- **Labeled** (if doing supervised learning): With clear target variables
- **Relevant**: Actually connected to the problem you're trying to solve
- **Balanced**: Avoiding over-representation of one category
- **Unbiased** (as much as possible): So it doesn't teach harmful patterns

In real life, almost no data starts this way. That's where preprocessing comes in.

Data Preprocessing and Cleaning

This is where many AI engineers spend most of their time—prepping data before it ever reaches a model.

Preprocessing tasks include:

- Removing duplicates
- Handling missing values
- Normalizing numeric fields

- Encoding categories into numbers
- Splitting into training, validation, and test sets

Clean data = better models. Period.

Importance of Bias and Fairness in Datasets

Even the best model will reflect the biases of its training data. If that data reflects historical inequalities or skewed sampling, the model can learn—and amplify—those patterns.

Examples:

- A hiring model trained mostly on male applicant resumes may prefer male candidates
- A facial recognition model trained on light-skinned faces may struggle with darker skin tones

Being a responsible AI engineer means checking your data—and your assumptions—for fairness and representativeness.

Wrapping Up

This chapter covered a lot—but everything here forms the backbone of what you'll build in future chapters. AI engineering combines theory, math, data, and code into systems that learn from experience.

Next up, we'll walk step by step through your first AI project: choosing a problem, training a model, and evaluating its performance.

Let's build something together.

3

Building Your First AI Models

You've explored how AI systems learn, what data they need, and the math that powers them. Now it's time to get your hands dirty. This chapter will walk you through your first AI project—from picking a problem to training a model and evaluating the results.

The best way to learn AI is by doing it. So think of this chapter as your first real test drive.

1. Choosing the Right Problem

Not every problem is a good fit for AI—and not every AI project needs to be complicated. Start small. Focus on learning the process, not building the next Google on your first try.

Defining a Problem Statement

The first step is to clearly articulate *what* you want your model to predict or classify. This is your **problem statement**.

A good one is:

- Specific
- Measurable
- Based on available data

Example: Predict whether a customer will cancel their subscription based on usage data.

Not great: Use AI to make our business more efficient.

Avoid vague or overly broad goals. A clear problem statement guides everything—from which data you need to which model you choose.

Understanding Input and Output

Every model takes an **input** and returns an **output**. Your job is to define both.

Let's say you're building a model to detect spam emails:

- **Input**: Email text
- **Output**: 1 if spam, 0 if not

Think of the input as your question and the output as your model's answer.

You also need to consider:

- Is this a **classification** problem (predict a category)?

- Or a **regression** problem (predict a number)?

Knowing the type of problem helps you choose the right algorithm.

Setting Realistic Expectations

Your first model won't be perfect—and that's okay.

Don't aim for 100% accuracy. Instead, focus on:

- Building a complete pipeline from data to prediction
- Understanding where the model performs well—and where it doesn't
- Learning how to interpret and improve your results

AI engineering is as much about **iteration** as innovation.

2. Model Development Workflow

Let's walk through the steps you'll follow in almost every machine learning project.

Data Collection and Labeling

You need data to train your model. You can:

- Download a public dataset (like from Kaggle, UCI, or data.gov)

- Scrape it from the web (ethically and legally!)
- Generate it yourself through logs or sensors
- Label it manually (especially for niche problems)

For supervised learning, your dataset needs **labels**—the correct answers the model will learn from. This could be:

- 0/1 for spam
- Star ratings for reviews
- Dollar values for housing prices

Model Selection and Training

You've got your data. Now it's time to choose a model.

If you're just starting out, stick with the basics:

- **Logistic regression**: Simple, fast, interpretable—great for binary classification
- **Decision trees**: Easy to visualize, can handle nonlinear data
- **k-Nearest Neighbors (k-NN)**: Simple to understand, good for classification
- **Linear regression**: For predicting continuous values

Using **Scikit-learn**, training a model looks like this:

```python
from sklearn.linear_model import LogisticRegression
model = LogisticRegression()
model.fit(X_train, y_train)
```

That's it—your model is trained. Now it's time to see how well it performs.

Evaluation and Performance Metrics

To know if your model is any good, you need to test it on data it hasn't seen before.

Common performance metrics:

- **Accuracy**: % of predictions that were correct
- **Precision**: % of predicted positives that were true positives
- **Recall**: % of actual positives that were correctly predicted
- **F1 Score**: Harmonic mean of precision and recall (good for imbalanced datasets)

And don't forget to split your data:

```python
from sklearn.model_selection import train_test_split
X_train, X_test, y_train, y_test = train_test_split(X, y, test_size=0.2)
```

Use your test set *only* to evaluate final performance—never to train or tune the model.

3. Tools for Beginners

You don't need a complex infrastructure to get started. These beginner-friendly tools will help you explore, build, and share your first projects.

Jupyter Notebooks and Google Colab

Jupyter Notebooks let you run code in chunks and mix it with text, charts, and images. Great for learning and prototyping.

Google Colab is a cloud-based version of Jupyter. Benefits:

- Free access to GPUs
- No installation required
- Easy sharing via links

You can start coding your first model today in Colab without installing anything.

Using Scikit-learn and TensorFlow

- **Scikit-learn** is perfect for beginners. It provides everything you need to train, test, and tune models like logistic regression, decision trees, and more.
- **TensorFlow** (and its high-level wrapper **Keras**) is a more advanced framework for deep learning.

Here's an example of a simple neural network with Keras:

```python
from tensorflow import keras
model = keras.Sequential([
    keras.layers.Dense(32, activation='relu'),
    keras.layers.Dense(1, activation='sigmoid')
])
model.compile(optimizer='adam', loss='binary_crossentropy')
model.fit(X_train, y_train, epochs=10)
```

It may look complex at first, but after a few projects, it'll feel natural.

Version Control with Git

Git helps you:

- Track your code changes
- Revert to earlier versions
- Work on experiments without breaking your main code
- Collaborate with others

Git + GitHub = your public AI portfolio.

Even for solo projects, Git is worth learning early. It's a hallmark of professional engineering.

Wrapping Up

You've just taken your first steps into actual model-building. You've learned how to define a problem, pick a model, train it, and evaluate it. You've also been introduced to tools that make all of this not only possible—but practical and efficient.

Remember: your first few models are like first drafts. Imperfect. Messy. But essential. With each one, you'll learn more about the data, the tools, and the real-world challenges of building intelligent systems.

In the next chapter, we'll move beyond clean datasets and tidy examples—and dive into the realities of **real-world data**: where to find it, how to clean it, and how to build pipelines that scale.

Let's keep going.

4

Working with Real-World Data

In theory, AI sounds sleek and seamless—data in, predictions out. But in reality? The data is messy. It's incomplete, inconsistent, unlabeled, unbalanced, and sometimes just plain weird.

Real-world AI projects don't begin with models. They begin with *data wrangling*—the unglamorous but absolutely essential process of finding, preparing, and managing the raw material that makes machine learning possible.

In this chapter, you'll learn how to find datasets, make them usable, and set up repeatable data workflows that scale.

1. Sourcing Datasets

Open Data Platforms and APIs

One of the best ways to get started is by tapping into public datasets. Here are some great places to explore:

- **Kaggle Datasets**: Thousands of curated datasets, plus kernels (sample notebooks) and competitions.
- **UCI Machine Learning Repository**: A classic resource with datasets used in academic studies.
- **Google Dataset Search**: A search engine just for datasets.
- **Government Portals**: data.gov (U.S.), data.gov.uk, and others host public data on everything from healthcare to agriculture.
- **APIs**: Services like Twitter, Reddit, Spotify, or OpenWeatherMap allow you to pull data in real-time. You'll often use Python libraries like requests, tweepy, or beautifulsoup4 to interact with them.

These sources offer labeled data for training, unlabeled data for exploration, and real-time feeds for live projects.

Building Your Own Dataset

Sometimes, the data you need doesn't exist—or isn't available in the form you want. In that case, you'll have to build your own.

You can:

- **Scrape websites** (using BeautifulSoup or Scrapy)

- **Collect data via forms, sensors, or apps**
- **Log user behavior in a product**
- **Label your own examples**

This gives you control—and the ability to solve unique or niche problems. Yes, it takes time. But custom datasets often lead to the most impactful results.

Privacy and Licensing Concerns

Just because data is online doesn't mean you can use it freely. Be aware of:

- **Copyright and licensing**: Some data can be used freely; others require attribution or restrict commercial use.
- **Terms of service**: Scraping a site might violate their policies.
- **Personally identifiable information (PII)**: Email addresses, phone numbers, and even combinations of non-sensitive data (like ZIP code + birthdate) can violate privacy laws like GDPR or HIPAA.

When in doubt: anonymize, minimize, and document.

2. Data Preprocessing Techniques

Once you've got the data, the real work begins. Preprocessing is where you clean it, shape it, and turn it into something your model can learn from.

Cleaning and Formatting Raw Data

Raw data is rarely tidy. Common issues include:

- Duplicates
- Missing values
- Inconsistent formatting
- Strange outliers
- Mismatched categories

Using Pandas, you can handle most cleaning tasks efficiently:

```python
import pandas as pd

df = pd.read_csv("your_data.csv")
df.drop_duplicates(inplace=True)
df.fillna(0, inplace=True)
df['category'] = df['category'].str.lower().str.strip()
```

Cleaning isn't glamorous, but it's what makes machine learning possible.

Feature Extraction and Selection

Not all columns in your data are useful—and some might even hurt your model.

Feature extraction creates new variables from existing ones. Examples:

- Converting a timestamp into "hour of day" or "day of week"
- Turning text into numeric vectors using NLP
- Aggregating user behavior logs into summary stats

Feature selection removes irrelevant or redundant variables. You can use:

- Correlation heatmaps
- Tree-based feature importance
- Recursive feature elimination

Good features make good models.

Dealing with Missing and Imbalanced Data

Real-world datasets often have gaps—and skew.

Missing data:

- Drop rows or columns (if few are affected)
- Fill in (impute) with the mean, median, or a model prediction
- Flag missingness as a feature (sometimes missing = signal)

Imbalanced data (e.g., 95% of your emails are *not* spam):

- Use different metrics (like F1 or AUC)
- Upsample minority class or downsample majority
- Try SMOTE (Synthetic Minority Over-sampling Technique)

Treat your data with care. Models trained on bad data can cause harm—or just perform poorly.

3. Data Pipelines

When you move beyond one-off notebooks, you'll need to **automate** your data workflows. That's where pipelines come in.

Automating Data Workflows

A data pipeline is a repeatable sequence of steps:

- Load data
- Clean it
- Transform features
- Save to disk or pass to a model

You can start with basic Python scripts, but as your projects grow, tools like **Airflow**, **Luigi**, or **Prefect** help you schedule and monitor jobs.

Think of a pipeline like an assembly line for data—automated, monitored, and version-controlled.

ETL (Extract, Transform, Load) Concepts

ETL is a concept borrowed from data engineering. It breaks your pipeline into three phases:

- **Extract**: Pull data from APIs, databases, CSV files, etc.
- **Transform**: Clean, filter, aggregate, normalize.
- **Load**: Save to a new format, database, or modeling environment.

A simple ETL process might:

- Pull yesterday's sales data
- Filter out refunds
- Calculate daily metrics
- Save the output to a database for dashboarding

You don't need to be a full-time data engineer—but understanding ETL makes your AI models much more scalable and reproducible.

Using Tools Like Airflow or Prefect

When you're ready to scale your workflows, tools like **Apache Airflow** and **Prefect** help you:

- Schedule recurring jobs (e.g., retrain your model every Sunday)
- Monitor task success/failure
- Define dependencies between steps
- Retry failed tasks automatically

These tools give you visibility and control over your data lifecycle.

A small project might not need them—but if your model is powering a product or running daily predictions, a pipeline framework is a must.

Wrapping Up

AI isn't built in the cloud. It's built in the *data*. And working with real-world data is messy, nonlinear, and full of surprises.

But that's where the magic happens.

If you can source high-quality data, clean it, engineer strong features, and build robust pipelines—you're already 70% of the way to a successful AI system.

In the next chapter, we'll explore how to move from experimentation to deployment. You'll learn what it takes to ship models into production—and keep them running smoothly over time.

Let's go.

5

Understanding AI Model Deployment

You've trained your model. It performs well. The graphs look good, the accuracy is solid. But now comes the big question: *how do you actually use it in the real world?*

Model deployment is about taking your model out of the notebook and into the hands of users, systems, and products. It's where machine learning stops being an academic exercise and starts delivering value.

In this chapter, you'll learn how deployment works, what tools are available, and how to manage the lifecycle of a model in production.

1. From Prototype to Production

Key Differences Between Testing and Deployment

In development, your model lives in a perfect little sandbox. You control the data, the timing, the environment. But production? That's a different world entirely.

Key differences:

- **Data shifts**: Users generate new kinds of data all the time
- **Performance demands**: Models must respond quickly under load
- **Monitoring and logging**: You can't inspect predictions by hand anymore
- **Reliability matters**: A single bad prediction in production can have consequences

Your job is to make sure the model performs just as well—or better—under pressure.

Challenges in Scaling AI Solutions

Scaling means making your model work for more users, more requests, and more data—without collapsing under the weight.

Common challenges:

- **Latency**: Can your model make predictions fast enough for real-time use?
- **Throughput**: Can it handle hundreds or thousands of requests per second?
- **Cost**: Are you running expensive computations

every time someone uses the app?

- **Infrastructure**: Does your system scale automatically? Can it recover from failure?

These are engineering problems—but solving them is what makes your AI usable and valuable.

Model Retraining and Monitoring

A model isn't "done" once it's deployed. Over time, its performance can drift as the data changes.

You'll need to:

- Collect fresh data
- Monitor prediction accuracy
- Detect changes in user behavior
- Retrain models regularly (weekly, monthly, or event-triggered)

This is often referred to as **ML lifecycle management**—and it's where MLOps (machine learning operations) comes in.

2. Deployment Platforms and Tools

Cloud Services (AWS, Azure, GCP)

The big cloud providers all offer end-to-end ML services.

- **Amazon Web Services (AWS)**: Includes Amazon SageMaker for training and deployment. Also offers Lambda (serverless) and EC2 (custom compute).
- **Google Cloud Platform (GCP)**: Features Vertex AI, AutoML, and native support for TensorFlow and TPUs.
- **Microsoft Azure**: Offers Azure Machine Learning Studio and powerful integration with enterprise tools.

Benefits of cloud platforms:

- On-demand scalability
- Built-in security and monitoring
- Easy integration with storage, databases, and APIs
- Access to specialized hardware (GPUs, TPUs)

If you're deploying a professional or customer-facing product, cloud hosting is almost always the way to go.

Containers and APIs (Docker, FastAPI)

To serve your model as a **web service**, you'll usually:

1. Wrap it in an **API**
2. Package it in a **container**

- **FastAPI**: A lightweight Python framework for building fast RESTful APIs. Great for serving models with minimal overhead.
- **Flask**: Another popular Python microframework—simple and reliable.
- **Docker**: Lets you package your app, model, and dependencies into a "container" that runs the same on any machine.

Basic deployment flow:

1. Save your model using joblib or pickle
2. Build an API that loads the model and returns predictions
3. Use Docker to containerize the API
4. Deploy to the cloud using a service like AWS ECS, Heroku, or Google Cloud Run

With a few lines of code, your model goes from "working on my laptop" to "live on the internet."

MLOps Basics

MLOps is like DevOps, but for machine learning. It's all about automating and managing the end-to-end ML workflow.

Core ideas:

- Version control for data, code, and models
- Automated training, testing, and deployment pipelines
- Continuous monitoring and logging
- Collaboration and reproducibility

Popular tools:

- **MLflow** for experiment tracking and model registry
- **Kubeflow** for managing ML pipelines in Kubernetes
- **Weights & Biases**, **Comet**, and **Neptune.ai** for logging and visualization

You don't need all this on day one—but understanding MLOps will prepare you to work on larger, more complex systems.

3. Keeping Models Alive

Deployment isn't the finish line—it's the beginning of a new phase. Live models need care, feeding, and monitoring.

Performance Monitoring and Metrics

After deployment, track:

- **Latency**: Time to return a prediction
- **Throughput**: Requests handled per second
- **Accuracy** (if ground truth is available post-prediction)
- **Error rates** and unusual outputs

Use logging tools to track predictions, inputs, and model behavior. Tools like **Prometheus**, **Grafana**, and **Datadog** can visualize and alert on key metrics.

Proactive monitoring = faster fixes and more reliable systems.

Updating and Versioning Models

When you retrain or tweak a model, treat it like software:

- Version your models (v1.0, v1.1, etc.)
- Use **A/B testing** to compare new and old

versions

- Deploy updates incrementally (e.g., 10% of users at first)

This avoids downtime and reduces the risk of performance regressions.

Avoiding Model Drift

Model drift happens when your model slowly stops working well due to changes in input data or real-world behavior.

Types:

- **Data drift**: Input features change (e.g., new slang in user reviews)
- **Concept drift**: Relationships change (e.g., customer behavior shifts after a major event)

How to manage drift:

- Monitor prediction distributions
- Set up alerts for performance drops
- Retrain frequently using recent data

Good drift detection means your model adapts—before it fails.

Wrapping Up

Deploying an AI model is a huge milestone—but it's not a solo task. It takes a team, a process, and the right tools to make it work in production.

As an AI engineer, your role is to make sure the model doesn't just *work*—but works reliably, safely, and at scale. You'll balance performance with cost, accuracy with speed, and predictions with people's trust.

In the next chapter, we'll shift gears and talk about something that touches *every* stage of AI development: **ethics and responsibility**.

Because the smarter our systems get, the more important it becomes to build them with care.

6

Ethics and Responsible AI

Artificial intelligence has the potential to help solve some of the world's biggest challenges—but only if we build it responsibly.

AI systems influence who gets a loan, which job candidates are interviewed, what news we see, and how we're treated by institutions. When these systems are designed thoughtfully, they can increase fairness and efficiency. But when they aren't? They can reinforce bias, invade privacy, and cause real harm.

In this chapter, we'll explore where ethical issues arise in AI, how to build systems that account for fairness and transparency, and what frameworks exist to help you build AI that earns—and deserves—trust.

1. Identifying Ethical Challenges

Bias in AI Systems

AI systems learn from data—and data reflects the world we live in. That world includes inequalities, stereotypes, and historical injustices. When unchecked, models can learn those patterns and replicate them.

Examples:

- Facial recognition systems that misidentify people of color at higher rates
- Hiring tools that downgrade resumes with traditionally female names
- Credit scoring models that penalize applicants from certain ZIP codes

Bias can sneak in through:

- Skewed datasets
- Incomplete features
- Labeling errors
- Hidden correlations that reflect societal bias

As an AI engineer, your job includes identifying potential sources of bias, testing for them, and mitigating them with both technical and design solutions.

Privacy Concerns and Data Misuse

AI systems often depend on **personal data**—emails, conversations, health records, location data. Used wisely, this can improve user experience. But used carelessly, it can violate privacy or even endanger users.

Key questions to ask:

- Was the data collected with informed consent?
- Could the system be misused to infer sensitive traits (e.g., sexual orientation, political views)?
- Are we storing more information than we need?

Privacy is not just a legal obligation—it's a matter of trust.

Algorithmic Transparency

Imagine being denied a loan or flagged by a security system and not knowing why. That's the problem with "black box" AI: decisions that are high-stakes, but impossible to explain.

Transparency matters because:

- People deserve to understand how decisions are made
- Engineers need to debug and validate behavior
- Regulators may require explainability for legal compliance

A good AI system doesn't just make predictions—it explains them.

2. Designing for Responsibility

Fairness and Accountability

Fairness isn't one-size-fits-all. What's "fair" in one context might not be in another. That's why you need to define fairness explicitly—and test for it throughout your project.

Fairness approaches include:

- **Demographic parity**: Equal outcomes across groups
- **Equal opportunity**: Equal true positive rates
- **Counterfactual fairness**: The prediction wouldn't change if a sensitive attribute (like gender or race) were changed

Choose a metric that aligns with your values and use tools (like Aequitas or IBM Fairness 360) to test your model.

Accountability means being clear about who is responsible when AI systems make mistakes or cause harm. Is it the data scientist? The business team? The software engineer?

You may not have the final say, but you *can* advocate for clarity and shared ownership.

Human-in-the-Loop Systems

Not every decision should be fully automated—especially in high-stakes settings like hiring, healthcare, or criminal justice.

Human-in-the-loop design means the AI supports a decision, but doesn't make it alone.

Examples:

- A radiologist reviews AI-suggested diagnoses
- A moderator double-checks AI-flagged social media posts
- A hiring manager sees AI-ranked resumes but makes the final call

This approach helps:

- Prevent automation bias
- Catch edge cases
- Increase accountability

AI should amplify human judgment—not replace it.

Explainable AI (XAI)

Explainable AI helps users, engineers, and regulators understand how and why a model made a decision.

Techniques include:

- **LIME** and **SHAP** for local feature attribution
- **Saliency maps** for visual models
- **Surrogate models** (simple models that approximate complex ones)

In regulated domains, explainability might be a legal requirement. In all domains, it builds trust and reveals hidden flaws.

Even with complex models, you can often offer simplified, intuitive explanations that answer user questions: *Why did I get this result? What could I change?*

3. Industry Guidelines and Frameworks

AI Ethics Principles from Major Organizations

Dozens of companies and organizations have published ethical guidelines for AI. While the wording varies, common principles include:

- **Fairness**: Avoid discrimination and bias
- **Transparency**: Explain how the system works
- **Privacy**: Protect user data
- **Accountability**: Assign responsibility
- **Safety**: Ensure the system won't cause harm

- **Human control**: Keep humans in the loop when needed

Examples:

- OECD AI Principles
- European Commission's Ethics Guidelines for Trustworthy AI
- Google's AI Principles
- IEEE's Ethically Aligned Design

These documents don't solve every problem—but they provide a strong foundation for responsible AI development.

Legal and Regulatory Considerations

AI is entering the realm of law—and engineers need to understand the basics.

Key frameworks include:

- **GDPR (General Data Protection Regulation)**: Gives users rights over their data and requires transparency in automated decisions (EU)
- **AI Act (EU)**: Proposes risk-based regulation of AI systems
- **California Consumer Privacy Act (CCPA)**:

Offers similar protections to GDPR

Regulations are evolving fast. Expect more laws that govern how AI can be used—and be ready to design systems that comply.

Building Trust Through Transparency

At the end of the day, ethics is about **trust**. If users don't trust your AI system, they won't use it—or worse, they'll use it and be harmed.

How to build trust:

- Clearly communicate how your model works
- Offer opt-outs when possible
- Document your data sources, decisions, and limitations
- Be open about uncertainty and risk

Some teams publish **model cards**—simple documentation about what the model does, how it was trained, and where it might fail. Others use **datasheets for datasets** to explain where training data came from and how it was labeled.

Transparency isn't just about compliance. It's about respect.

Wrapping Up

Ethics in AI isn't just something you bolt on at the end. It's something you build in—at every stage.

As an AI engineer, you're not just writing code. You're shaping how machines make decisions, how people interact with those machines, and how those systems affect the world.

That's a powerful responsibility. Embrace it.

In the next chapter, we'll return to the practical side of things—focusing on the **core tools** that every AI engineer should know.

7

Core Tools Every AI Engineer Should Know

Building AI isn't just about knowing the concepts—it's about knowing the tools. Just like a carpenter needs a hammer and saw, an AI engineer needs the right languages, libraries, environments, and infrastructure.

This chapter introduces the key tools you'll use throughout your AI journey. Some are great for getting started. Others are used to build, test, and deploy models at scale. All of them are worth knowing.

1. Programming Languages and Libraries

Python Essentials

Python is the lingua franca of AI. It's readable, flexible, and has a massive ecosystem of libraries that make machine learning easy and fast to implement.

Core skills you'll need:

- Writing functions and classes
- Using list comprehensions and lambda functions
- Handling exceptions
- Reading/writing files
- Importing and using packages

If you're new to Python, focus on learning:

- for and while loops
- if statements
- Lists, dictionaries, tuples
- Writing and importing modules

Python also supports object-oriented programming, which becomes more important as your projects grow in size and complexity.

TensorFlow, PyTorch, and Keras

These are the go-to frameworks for deep learning.

- **TensorFlow** (by Google): A powerful, scalable platform with strong production support. Great for deploying models on the web or mobile.
- **PyTorch** (by Meta): More intuitive and Pythonic. Popular in research and for rapid

prototyping.

- **Keras**: A high-level API for building and training models, often used with TensorFlow under the hood.

A simple Keras example:

```python
from tensorflow import keras
model = keras.Sequential([
    keras.layers.Dense(64, activation='relu'),
    keras.layers.Dense(1, activation='sigmoid')
])
model.compile(optimizer='adam', loss='binary_crossentropy')
model.fit(X_train, y_train, epochs=10)
```

These tools let you build neural networks without diving deep into the math of backpropagation. But as you gain experience, you can customize and optimize everything under the hood.

OpenCV and spaCy for Vision/NLP

If you're working with **images**, use:

- **OpenCV**: For basic image processing, object detection, video capture, and more.

For **language tasks**, use:

- **spaCy**: An NLP library for tokenization, entity recognition, and syntactic parsing.
- **NLTK**: A beginner-friendly toolkit for working with human language data.

- **Hugging Face Transformers**: Pretrained models like BERT and GPT for advanced NLP tasks.

With these tools, you can build apps that "see" and "read" like humans—and do it fast.

2. Development Environments

IDEs and Notebooks (VS Code, Jupyter)

Where you write your code matters.

- **Jupyter Notebooks**: Perfect for experimentation and exploration. You can run code in cells, visualize outputs instantly, and add markdown notes.

- **Google Colab**: A free, cloud-based Jupyter environment with GPU access.

- **VS Code**: A lightweight, flexible code editor. Great for building larger projects and working with files, virtual environments, and Git.

Jupyter is ideal for rapid development. VS Code is ideal for scaling projects.

Many engineers use both—starting in notebooks, then migrating to scripts or modules in VS Code.

Version Control with Git and GitHub

As your projects grow, version control becomes essential. Git helps you:

- Track changes
- Revert to previous versions
- Experiment without fear
- Collaborate with others

GitHub is the cloud-based home for your repositories. It's where employers and collaborators can see your work.

Common Git commands:

```bash
git init
git add .
git commit -m "Initial commit"
git push origin main
```

Version control is like a time machine for your code. Don't build without it.

Package Managers and Virtual Environments

Different projects require different libraries—and different library versions. That's where package managers and environments come in.

- **pip**: The standard Python package manager.
- **virtualenv / venv**: Create isolated environments for each project.

- **conda**: A popular alternative, especially in data science workflows. Manages both packages and environments.

Using environments prevents the dreaded "dependency hell" and makes your projects portable and reproducible.

3. Infrastructure and Cloud

Using GPUs and TPUs

Training deep learning models on a laptop CPU is like trying to run a marathon in flip-flops—it'll work, but you'll suffer.

GPUs (Graphics Processing Units) massively speed up training by handling matrix operations in parallel. Use them for:

- Neural networks
- Image processing
- Large-scale batch training

TPUs (Tensor Processing Units) are Google's custom chips for TensorFlow. Fast and efficient, but a bit more niche.

You can access GPUs for free (limited usage) via:

- **Google Colab**

- **Kaggle Notebooks**

Or pay for more power with cloud platforms.

Cloud Platforms for Training and Hosting

Cloud platforms give you access to powerful resources, scalability, and integrated services.

Top platforms:

- **AWS (Amazon Web Services)**
- **Google Cloud Platform (GCP)**
- **Microsoft Azure**

These let you:

- Train models on GPU clusters
- Store and serve datasets
- Deploy APIs or full-stack apps
- Monitor performance at scale

If you're planning to turn your model into a product, learning cloud deployment is key.

Scaling and Cost Management

Cloud power comes at a price. Smart engineers manage resources wisely.

Tips:

- Use **spot instances** for cheaper compute
- Shut down unused instances
- Use **batch processing** where real-time isn't needed
- Optimize model size with quantization or pruning

Scalability is about delivering performance while staying efficient and cost-effective.

Wrapping Up

You don't need to master every tool today—but learning how they fit together will make you faster, more effective, and more confident.

Start simple. Use Jupyter. Learn Git. Experiment with Scikit-learn and Colab. Then gradually move into TensorFlow, Docker, cloud services, and MLOps.

AI engineering is about continuous learning—and these tools are your launchpad.

In the next chapter, we'll explore what it takes to turn your skills into a career. Whether you're just starting out or looking to level up, we'll walk through certifications, portfolios, and real-world job paths.

Let's go.

8

Career Pathways in AI Engineering

So, you've been learning, experimenting, and building AI projects—and now you're wondering, *What's next?*

Whether you're just starting out, switching careers, or looking to grow within your current role, the field of AI engineering offers a wide range of opportunities. But with so many job titles, bootcamps, courses, and career advice floating around, it can be hard to know where to begin.

In this chapter, we'll break down your career roadmap—how to learn, what to build, where to work, and how to stand out.

1. Education and Certification

Degrees vs. Bootcamps vs. Self-Study

There are many ways into AI engineering—and no single "right" path. What matters most is your ability to apply what you've learned and demonstrate it through real projects.

Degrees

- Pros: Deep foundations in math, algorithms, and systems; credibility; access to research labs and internships
- Cons: Expensive and time-consuming (2–4 years)
- Best for: Those pursuing academia, research, or long-term roles in enterprise/FAANG settings

Bootcamps

- Pros: Focused, fast-paced, and hands-on; industry-relevant projects
- Cons: Expensive; quality varies widely
- Best for: Career switchers and those seeking a guided transition into tech

Self-Study

- Pros: Flexible, low-cost or free, learn at your own pace
- Cons: Requires discipline and structure
- Best for: Independent learners who enjoy project-based growth

Great self-study resources include:

- Coursera (Andrew Ng's ML & Deep Learning

Specialization)

- edX, Udacity, Fast.ai
- YouTube tutorials, blogs, and GitHub projects

No matter which path you take, *projects and practical experience* are what employers look for most.

Top Certifications and Programs

Certifications don't guarantee a job—but they can help your resume stand out, especially for recruiters screening non-traditional candidates.

Popular options:

- **AWS Certified Machine Learning – Specialty**
- **Google Cloud Professional ML Engineer**
- **Microsoft Azure AI Engineer Associate**
- **DeepLearning.AI TensorFlow Developer Certificate**
- **IBM AI Engineering Professional Certificate (Coursera)**

Choose programs that include hands-on labs and build real-world skills—not just multiple-choice quizzes.

Building a Learning Roadmap

Start here:

1. **Python programming basics**
2. **Data manipulation and visualization** (Pandas, NumPy, Matplotlib)
3. **ML fundamentals** (supervised learning, model evaluation)
4. **Build mini-projects** with Scikit-learn or TensorFlow
5. **Explore deep learning and NLP/vision applications**
6. **Deploy your models (e.g., FastAPI + Docker or Streamlit)**
7. **Learn cloud tools (AWS/GCP) and Git for collaboration**
8. **Create a portfolio to show it all off**

Learning AI is a journey. Pace yourself—but keep moving forward.

2. Building a Portfolio

Types of Projects That Stand Out

Employers want to see evidence that you can solve real problems. Great portfolios include projects that are:

- **Well-defined**: Clear problem statement and outcome
- **End-to-end**: Includes data prep, modeling, evaluation, and deployment
- **Useful or creative**: Something people can engage with or relate to
- **Documented and shareable**: So others can understand your thought process

Project ideas:

- Movie recommender system
- AI-powered resume analyzer
- Sentiment analysis on Twitter data
- Image classifier for plant diseases
- Chatbot that answers FAQs from your favorite book or brand

One great project is better than five unfinished ones.

Documenting and Sharing Your Work

Every project should include:

- A **README.md** that explains what it is, why it matters, and how to run it
- Screenshots, diagrams, or a short demo video
- Code that is clean, commented, and well-organized
- A write-up on Medium, Substack, or Dev.to that describes your approach

Post your work on:

- **GitHub**: Your professional coding portfolio
- **LinkedIn**: Share updates and build visibility
- **Personal blog or portfolio site** (optional but powerful)

Tell the story behind your project. Show your thought process. That's what employers remember.

Open Source Contributions

Contributing to open source is a fantastic way to:

- Build real-world experience
- Collaborate with others
- Grow your network
- Give back to the community

Start with:

- Improving documentation
- Fixing bugs
- Creating tutorials
- Participating in issues or discussions

Look for beginner-friendly tags like good first issue or help wanted on GitHub. Projects like Scikit-learn, Hugging Face, and Streamlit are welcoming and active.

3. Job Roles and Opportunities

AI Engineer vs. ML Engineer vs. Data Scientist

These titles often overlap—but here's a quick breakdown:

- **AI Engineer**: Focuses on building intelligent systems, often including deep learning, NLP, or vision tasks. Tends to be application-focused.

- **ML Engineer**: Designs, builds, and deploys machine learning models. Strong on infrastructure, data pipelines, and MLOps.
- **Data Scientist**: Explores and analyzes data to extract insights. May build models, but often more focused on experimentation and business value.

Other roles:

- **Data Engineer**: Prepares and maintains data infrastructure.
- **Applied Researcher**: Works at the intersection of engineering and new model development.
- **AI Product Manager**: Leads strategy and development for AI-powered features or tools.

Read job descriptions carefully—not just titles. The actual work varies widely between companies.

In-Demand Industries and Domains

AI is transforming nearly every sector. Top industries hiring AI talent include:

- **Healthcare**: Diagnostics, drug discovery, personalized treatment
- **Finance**: Fraud detection, risk modeling, trading algorithms

- **Retail/E-commerce**: Recommendation engines, demand forecasting
- **Transportation**: Route optimization, self-driving vehicles
- **Agriculture**: Crop analysis, smart irrigation
- **Media**: Personalization, content generation
- **EdTech**: Adaptive learning, AI tutors

You don't need to be an expert in every field. But learning a little domain context can help you stand out and build smarter solutions.

Interview Tips and Technical Assessments

AI job interviews usually involve:

- **Coding questions** (Python, data structures, algorithms)
- **ML theory** (bias/variance, overfitting, model types)
- **Practical problems** (build a simple classifier, analyze a dataset)
- **Behavioral questions** (collaboration; dealing with failure)

Tips:

- Practice coding on LeetCode or HackerRank
- Review ML concepts and evaluation metrics
- Walk through your portfolio projects—explain decisions, trade-offs, and results
- Ask thoughtful questions: "How is AI used in your company's products?" or "What's the team's MLOps stack?"

Remember, interviews are a two-way street. You're also assessing *them*.

Wrapping Up

AI engineering is a dynamic, creative, and high-impact career path. And the good news? There's never been a better time to get started.

Whether you're learning on your own, taking a course, or applying for your first job, focus on *doing the work*. Build projects. Solve problems. Share your story.

In the next chapter, we'll zoom out and see AI in the wild—with **real-world case studies**, from virtual assistants to healthcare breakthroughs. You'll learn what works, what breaks, and how to learn from both.

Let's keep going.

9

Case Studies and Real-World Applications

Learning the theory is important. Building your own projects is even better. But one of the best ways to become a smarter AI engineer is to study what others have done—especially when things didn't go as planned.

In this chapter, we'll explore real-world examples of AI in action: from everyday products you use to high-stakes industries like healthcare and finance. You'll see how AI models are built, deployed, scaled—and how they're refined based on feedback and failure.

1. AI in Everyday Life

Recommendation Systems

Every time you watch a show on Netflix, shop on Amazon, or listen to a song on Spotify, you're interacting with a recommendation engine. These systems use machine learning to predict what you'll like next based on your past behavior, the behavior of others, and metadata about the content.

Example:

Spotify's Discover Weekly combines collaborative filtering, content-based filtering, and natural language processing to create highly personalized playlists. It even scans music blogs and lyrics to capture taste patterns.

Key takeaway: Recommendation systems thrive on **scale** and **feedback loops**. The more data they get, the better they get—until they overfit and start suggesting the same things. Great systems balance personalization with diversity.

Virtual Assistants and Chatbots

From Siri and Alexa to customer service bots, virtual assistants use natural language processing (NLP) and speech recognition to understand queries and provide responses.

Example:

Gmail's Smart Reply uses a lightweight neural network to suggest short replies based on context. It's fast, doesn't interrupt the user experience, and learns from your writing style.

Key takeaway: The best NLP tools are **invisible**—they assist without overwhelming. They don't need to be perfect. They just need to save time and fit the user's expectations.

Smart Devices and IoT

AI also powers your thermostat, your smart speaker, and even your vacuum. These devices use AI to:

- Detect motion or voice
- Learn routines
- Respond to changing environments

Example:

Nest Thermostat uses reinforcement learning to adapt heating and cooling schedules based on user preferences, local weather, and real-time sensor data.

Key takeaway: AI doesn't need to be flashy. Some of the most useful models run quietly in the background—adjusting, learning, and improving over time.

2. Industry Use Cases

Healthcare Diagnostics

AI is transforming diagnostics by identifying patterns that humans might miss.

Example:

DeepMind's AI for eye disease diagnosis, developed

with Moorfields Eye Hospital, can detect over 50 retinal diseases from 3D scans with expert-level accuracy—and explain its reasoning to doctors.

Key takeaway: **Explainability** is crucial in healthcare. Doctors need to trust the system's recommendations and understand the logic behind them.

Caution: Models trained on limited or biased data may underperform on certain demographics—leading to misdiagnoses and inequality in care.

Financial Forecasting

Banks and financial firms use AI to:

- Predict loan defaults
- Detect fraud
- Automate trading
- Optimize customer service

Example:

PayPal's fraud detection system uses real-time anomaly detection models trained on millions of transactions per day. It prioritizes precision—flagging only what's truly suspicious.

Key takeaway: In high-volume, high-stakes industries, **false positives and false negatives** can be very costly. It's not just about accuracy—it's about the right kind of accuracy.

Autonomous Vehicles

Self-driving cars rely on multiple AI systems working together:

- **Computer vision** for object detection
- **Sensor fusion** for combining radar, LiDAR, and cameras
- **Reinforcement learning** for route planning and decision-making

Example:

Waymo's autonomous vehicles have driven millions of miles on public roads, using AI to navigate traffic, avoid obstacles, and make human-like driving decisions.

Key takeaway: Real-world environments are unpredictable. Models must be **robust**, **real-time**, and **fail-safe**—with fallbacks in case something goes wrong.

3. Lessons from Real Projects

What Went Right—and Wrong

What went right:

- **Gmail Smart Compose**: It started small, learned

from real user data, and improved gradually. It didn't try to replace writing—just assist it.

- **Netflix's recommendation engine**: Combines multiple models, real-time feedback, and editorial curation to avoid "filter bubble" fatigue.

What went wrong:

- **Microsoft Tay**: A Twitter chatbot that learned from user interaction—and was quickly corrupted by trolls. Within hours, it began posting offensive content and had to be shut down.

Lesson: **Reinforcement learning in the wild** needs constraints and guardrails.

- **COMPAS algorithm**: A criminal justice risk model found to be racially biased due to skewed historical data. Despite being widely used in sentencing and bail decisions, it lacked transparency and fairness.

Lesson: A model's predictions are only as fair as its **training data and evaluation criteria**.

Scaling Challenges

Small models in notebooks are easy. But what happens when your model is used by thousands—or millions—of users?

Challenges include:

- Model latency under load
- Retraining on fresh data without downtime
- Monitoring drift and performance
- Debugging in production

Solutions:

- Use cloud deployment and container orchestration (e.g., Kubernetes)
- Automate your training and deployment pipeline (MLOps)
- Track user feedback and prediction quality over time

Think of your model like software—it needs updates, testing, and logs.

User Feedback and Iteration

The real world is the ultimate test—and your users are your best QA team.

Good AI teams:

- Log and analyze user feedback
- Run A/B tests to compare model versions
- Use human-in-the-loop systems for sensitive decisions

- Embrace iteration: build, test, learn, repeat

Example:

Duolingo's AI adapts lessons based on user behavior. They run experiments constantly—measuring retention, satisfaction, and learning outcomes to refine their recommendation algorithms.

Wrapping Up

Real-world AI is not about perfection. It's about progress.

Projects succeed when teams:

- Start simple and build iteratively
- Monitor for problems and bias
- Involve users in the loop
- Stay transparent about limitations

In the final chapter, we'll turn our eyes to the horizon—exploring the **future of AI engineering**, emerging trends, and how you can stay curious and relevant in a field that never stands still.

10

The Future of AI Engineering

The field of AI moves fast. What was groundbreaking last year is now baseline. What's experimental today may be essential tomorrow.

But in all this change, one thing remains true: the future of AI isn't just about technology. It's about the people who build it—and how they choose to use it.

In this final chapter, we'll explore the biggest trends shaping the future of AI engineering, the role engineers will play in guiding that future, and how to keep growing—long after you close this book.

1. Emerging Trends

Generative AI and Large Language Models

AI is no longer just about *recognizing* patterns—it's about *creating*.

Generative AI systems can produce:

- Text (e.g., ChatGPT, Claude, Gemini)

- Images (e.g., DALL·E, Midjourney, Stable Diffusion)
- Music, video, and even code

They rely on **large language models (LLMs)** and other foundation models trained on vast datasets. These models can:

- Write stories, summarize documents, answer questions
- Generate Python code or SQL queries
- Translate between languages and formats

Opportunities:

- Creative tools, automation, personal assistants
- Customer service bots that actually help
- Education, research, and writing support

Challenges:

- Hallucinations (making things up)
- Data privacy and copyright
- Misinformation and bias

As an engineer, you'll need to know how to work with LLMs, fine-tune them, evaluate them—and use them responsibly.

AI at the Edge and On-Device Learning

The future of AI isn't just in the cloud. It's in your pocket, your car, and your watch.

Edge AI brings models to the device, instead of sending data to the cloud. This is faster, more private, and more reliable for:

- Mobile apps
- Wearables
- Smart appliances
- Drones and robots

New tools allow for **model compression**, **quantization**, and **on-device inference** using tools like TensorFlow Lite, Core ML, or PyTorch Mobile.

Expect to see more models running locally—especially as privacy concerns grow and devices become more powerful.

Multimodal AI Systems

Humans experience the world through many senses—sight, sound, touch, language. The future of AI is **multimodal**: combining different types of input and output to create more natural, flexible systems.

Multimodal AI can:

- Take in images *and* questions (e.g., "What is this person holding?")
- Analyze video, audio, and transcripts together
- Power assistants that see, hear, and speak like a human

These systems are already emerging in tools like GPT-4 with vision, and they're reshaping how we interact with machines.

2. The Role of Engineers in Shaping the Future

Creating Inclusive and Global AI

Most AI today is trained on data from a few dominant regions and languages. That creates blind spots—and leaves billions of people underserved.

Engineers can:

- Build models for underrepresented languages and dialects
- Translate research into accessible tools
- Use local data sources to solve local problems
- Partner with communities to design for real needs

AI should be a global movement—not just a Western export.

Building Systems That Evolve

Today's AI systems are mostly static. You train a model, you deploy it, and maybe you retrain it once in a while.

Tomorrow's systems will:

- Learn continuously from new data
- Personalize in real time
- Self-correct and adapt to new goals
- Monitor their own performance

This requires a mindset shift. You're not just building a one-time model. You're designing a living system.

That means thinking long-term about:

- Model versioning
- Feedback loops
- Safety and failover
- Lifespan and decay

The future belongs to flexible, adaptive systems—and the engineers who know how to build them.

Leading Innovation Responsibly

The decisions you make as an engineer have ripple effects. What you build—and how you build it—can shape:

- Who gets access to opportunity
- How people are treated by institutions
- What knowledge is shared or hidden
- How power is distributed in society

You don't need to have all the answers. But you do need to ask the questions:

- Who could be harmed by this model?
- What assumptions are baked into the data?
- Is the goal of this project aligned with the public good?
- Am I being transparent about the system's limitations?

Responsible innovation is not a constraint. It's a compass.

3. Becoming a Lifelong Learner

Staying Up-to-Date with Research

AI research moves fast. New architectures, datasets, and breakthroughs are published every day. You don't need to read every paper—but you should stay curious.

How to keep up:

- **arXiv.org**: Open-access research preprints
- **Papers with Code**: Combines papers, metrics, and code repos
- **The Batch** (newsletter from Andrew Ng)
- **DeepLearning.AI**, **Hugging Face blog**, **Distill.pub**

Follow the trends—but don't get overwhelmed. Learn what you need, when you need it.

Following Thought Leaders and Communities

The AI community is wide—and welcoming.

Follow thought leaders like:

- Andrew Ng
- Fei-Fei Li

- Yann LeCun
- Lex Fridman
- Rachel Thomas (Fast.ai)

And join communities:

- GitHub (follow projects and contributors)
- Twitter/X and LinkedIn (for news and ideas)
- Reddit (r/MachineLearning, r/DataScience)
- AI Discord groups and local meetups

Engaging with others keeps you connected—and helps you grow faster.

Keeping Curiosity Alive

The most powerful thing you can do? Stay curious.

Tinker with a new tool. Try a weird idea. Read outside your domain. Ask "what if?" questions. Follow a rabbit hole.

Some of the most impactful AI projects started as passion projects, side experiments, or unexpected collaborations.

You don't have to know where you're going yet. Just keep exploring.

Final Thoughts

You made it to the end of this book—but this is just the beginning of your journey.

You now understand the foundations of AI engineering:

- What AI is and how it works
- How to build models from scratch
- How to work with real data
- How to deploy, monitor, and maintain systems
- How to think about ethics, impact, and responsibility
- What tools, jobs, and communities will help you thrive

And most importantly, you know how to keep learning.

So go build something. Try. Fail. Try again. Share what you learn. Ask good questions. Stay humble. Stay hopeful. Stay human.

The future of AI is in your hands.

About the author

James Douglas is a writer and researcher based in Nashville, Tennessee. He enjoys exploring topics like artificial intelligence, fitness, and personal growth, with a focus on making complex ideas practical and accessible. James also writes books fueled by personal passion, aiming to inspire and empower readers in every season of life.

www.ingramcontent.com/pod-product-compliance
Lightning Source LLC
LaVergne TN
LVHW022308200926
848481LV00004B/1242